D1707461

The
WINDOW

The **WINDOW**

poems: 1998-2012

DAVID ST. JOHN

ARCTOS PRESS

The Window © 2014 by David St. John

First Edition

ISBN No.: 9780972538404

Library of Congress Control Number: 2014900286
Library of Congress Cataloging in Publication Data
1. Poetry 2. St. John, David — Poetry 3. United States —
21st Century — Poetry

Book Design by Tania Baban, Conflux Press

Cover image: © James Welling, "Santa Monica, 1978."
Used by permission of the artist.

Author photograph by Roger Snider

Printed in U.S.A.

Published by Arctos Press,
P.O. Box 401 Sausalito, California 94966
arctospress.com   Runes@aol.com

ARCTOS PRESS

for CB Follett & Susan Terris

CONTENTS

❧ *LOST LEAVES*

ACKNOWLEDGEMENTS

Aperçus Quarterly: Song of the Lost Peridot; The Last Naked Troubadour; The Black Slip

Burnside Review: Epiphanies; The Aurora of the Blind Dog

Gulf Coast: Torches

Poetry International: Velvet Aurora

Runes: Sonnet of the Monastic Refugee

Specs: Renaissance Willows

Spillway: The Window; High Street

The Ohio Review: Wisdom's Shadow; Focus; Of Fashion; Homecoming; Her Painting; Sunflowers; Classicism; Black Feathers; Waiting; Veils; Another Kiss

The poem "Automatic Autumn" first appeared on *The Best American Poetry* blog, edited by David Lehman.

The poem "Dijon" first appeared in the anthology, *Poets On Place,* edited by W. T. Pfefferle, Utah State University Press (2005).

The poems: "Her Painting;" and "Another Kiss" also appeared in *The New Bread Loaf Anthology of Contemporary American Poetry,* edited by Michael Collier and Stanley Plumly, Bread Loaf Writers Conference/Middlebury (1999)

"The Window" was commissioned by The Museum of Contemporary Art, Los Angeles for *This Language of Image,* new poems written in response to specific works in the exhibition, *Conceptualism in California from the Permanent Collection* (2008).

The poems in the section *Quechua Songs* were written to be part of a collaborative project (with master printmaker Holly Downing) entitled, *Peruvian Portals*, a fine press folio of poems and mezzotints. Selected poems and all of Holly Downing's mezzotints were also included in a group show at The USC Fisher Museum of Art, *Drawn to Language* (2013).

THE WINDOW

You could be anywhere, almost anywhere at all,

In almost any city & almost any abandoned life — but
You are here, standing again outside the house where she
Lived, looking up at her third floor apartment with its square
Corner tower & narrow windows, where you'd sit
At night, reading at a small table while she painted her huge,
Savage canvasses in the bare white living room she'd
Cluttered with drop sheets, buckets & brushes, scattered tubes
Of oils. Sex always smelled like espresso mixed with turpentine,
Like night-booming jasmine & Coltrane. Of course, you could be
Anywhere, but you are here, not even knowing if she's still
Living there, it's been so many years now since you
Walked out on her & left for the trenches of Manhattan —
A shadow steps first into & then out of the light, the soft
Brilliant rectangles of light framed by those corner windows . . .
& then, there's nothing except your emptiness, & the shadow
That might or might not have been hers. You could be anywhere.

You could be home.

after James Welling

1

❧ HIGH STREET

DIJON

The TGV sliced through the pulsing mustard fields

On its way from Paris to Nice
                        Where he would meet her for lunch
At last after the months of calls & letters

& they'd walk along the Promenade des Anglais

While she explained again all of those things
He could understand really no better walking alongside her

Than he could from his apartment off the Rue de Bac
That is: all of those reasons he no longer stood
Within the frame of her future

No longer remained the body she preferred to all other bodies

& now the sun seemed to scour the sand of the raw beaches
Below their old café with a blade as dulled

& yellowed as the fat knife she'd angled across her plate

SONG OF THE LOST PERIDOT

After Isabella spilled
Green ink along her hands & asked so solemnly
That everyone look away
Even her lover hid behind
The damask curtains & that little fingernail scratch
Of emerald along his cheek

& her wristlets of strung peridots
Were enough to make the late swollen olives tremble
In the orchard enough
To smear shut
The grappa-lit mouths of the neighbors & other gossips
& as the cello

Began playing in a distant *stanza*
The night again filled with rumor & those rumors filled
With light & the credenza
Itself filled with warm bread
& those last flaming ribbons of lace unraveled in her hand
& seven yellow stone towers

Began rising above
The fields outside of Ferrara & it was a time of
Endless courtliness
A time when Isabella
& her lover stood wrapped in the twin carapace of their own
Lizard-raw skins

& in your own hurried
Letter to Fiesole I remember your description of the twilight
Growing as vague
as a Madonna
& everywhere such sketches of lurid envy betrayed the craftsman's
Sturdy ground

But I stood in my own
Cold shadow thinking I might look beyond the swaying candles
Of the cypress
Outside her window
Yet it all seemed something I could have left only yesterday
As she arose

Like a little scrub-flag
Of instinct repeatedly saying *Non ancora non ancora*
Caro mia

THE LAST NAKED TROUBADOUR

I had supposed
His naked touch would reward you with its skin
Of sweetness
Rolled into your bowl
I had supposed the virginal night might console you
With bleeding eyes or

His nipples staring
Right through your heart (he'd said: *Milady*) singing
Beyond the unbound lace of
Any amorous bride
& let that place which is private rest as still as dust
Beyond your simplest

Imaginings & when
You consider the path that your thin knife describes
Along the wild arc
Of the troubadour's ribs
(The last of his kind sighs) think now of the sinew of his
Glance & of the muscles

Of his back & why

You love the absurd detail of his body washed in oils

As when you're rising

Like the dying ash blown awake

By the wind again as those wet blossoms along your thighs

Begin to dry just like

The prayers of a final echo or

The eloquent sadness of the dead or the reasons you wail

In the black riot of your bed

EPIPHANIES

Along the delicate scrollwork of her shoulders
Seven sentences of fear

Beneath the cardinal tides of the morning
The white crocuses had fallen just as beneath the majestic

Fronds of the palms lay the litany of Orphic psalms
All of it felt like a window onto my own grave

All of it rippled like the soft gaze of Athena I could not hold
In my precious self-regard

It was then the caramel-colored skeletons arose
Vigilant sentinels of the long-deliberated past

Those little Dada-lessons of the forgetful heart

THE AURORA OF THE BLIND DOG

Her hair was Italian & thicker than night
In the eyes of a blind dog

Even the nuclear harness of her blouse
Seemed to suggest something being torn

From a final universal truth

& of all the shopkeepers along all the streets
Of all the time-honored oracles

Holding their futures like tickets to the sullen sky
Only I the amnesiac of the moment was allowed

To imagine my life without her
As hearing a tune of ancient import I grew as lonely

As the last book of the future thrust open by knives

TORCHES

It was startling of course

To come upon you that way as I turned the corner

Of the garden path

& quite suddenly

You were there a torch in each hand your silk dress

Rippling with scars & crescents

As the torches' light beat

Along each of your cheeks & you said   *Come back with me*

& slowly we wound our way

Through those rainy hedges

Back to the party still murmuring from the dark patio

You'd filled with fake Roman statuary

& iced buckets of local wines

& with your arms held high above you touching the head

Of one torch to the other

Framing your face

In a pyramid of light   a stutter of applause ran

Through your guests as the smoke

Coiled over you like a woven crown

Then all in one movement you planted the hilt of each torch

Into the black earth

Of the broken urns beside us

& slowly turned to me your mouth still hard & flushed

By the heat of all those things

That the night

Had promised & all of those familiar promises I knew were

Yet to come

(Sicily)

THE BLACK SLIP

A black slip
Draped over the bare hanger she'd hung on
The dulled metal oval
Above the ice-white
Claw-footed porcelain tub
Clear drops gathering at the slip's

Dark hem dripping
One by one into the peeling white-washed dory
Of the old tub
& the slip itself was
The rare obsidian shadow of her own sculpted torso
Its silk sheen surpassing

Even the jet spines
Of her mother's beloved fan or the black agate
Of her father's solitary ring . . . .
It was the shadow
She'd so carefully stepped out of last evening
As he slept

Standing for a moment
Naked & alone beneath the nimbus of the overhead bulb
Bare & luminous — as she lifted
Her arms & breasts as if
In ritual supplication — as he slept on unknowingly
Her simple shadow

Collapsing again her fading
Resolve slowly stripped of its desire the fire
Again now white as ash
As her pale skin white
As that cold negative of breath she so slowly

So deliberately
& wholly has slipped once again
Within . . . .

VELVET AURORA

The bird on the walk unrolled his velvet jacket

& everything he saw he believed
Juliette stood beside Orpheus thinking only of her soul

& the way it always shivered in the shape of a pine

& everywhere *everywhere* the dark licked its lips again
& everywhere lilies lifted their faces

To the flames of hummingbirds just as

Everywhere there arose a sense of pure design
& all the songs & all the hymns were sung again

Beyond the velvet shadows of earthly love

SONNET OF THE MONASTIC REFUGEE

There was an albino lion quite famous
Throughout all of Paris as was the sight of

His mistress walking him to & fro
Under the long windows of Montparnasse

& they lived together in the bald desires of opium

& they were only a momentary ellipse in the life
Of the monk . . . the way his map of the Americas

Had unfolded beneath her warm lace gloves
(O my lost Conquistador!) as she praised

A sudden gust of spring air — & the monk stood
Silently beside his highly bred roses

Each reflecting (he said) only a murderous faith
& a constant if yet luminous

Despair

RENAISSANCE WILLOWS

Where was the lush breath of the peat
Where were the flakes of her silence falling

Where was the minstrel you fucked that minstrel of the sky
Beneath the willows & his flowing braids

Where was that famous bourgeois moment
Where was the algebra of his late late life

Where was the child's rattle of last farewells
Where was the refuge beyond the silver moors

Where was the one moon
Where was that couple walking solemnly along the pier

Where was the chameleon dressed like a Medici prince
Where was the snow & its simple mind

Where was the diamond dragonfly hanging around her neck
Where were the thistles by the sea & her thorn-spiked passions

Where were the inky maidens encircling the red clay vase
Where was the wreath of jasmine jealousy

Where was her Lourdes morning & the falcon falling
Where was the gale of the night & the Provençal light

Where was Venus rising in the palm of my left hand
Where was the weary mistress come home at last

HIGH STREET

We'd always meet at the café
There at the intersection of inscription & possibility
A lot of nonsense got said
& a lot of hopes
Got stirred like sugar yet it was I confess so satisfying
To be so indolent & young

So persuaded by our passports
To notoriety & so confident of the bullshit we'd write
So contemptuous of the fossils
Reviewing other fossils
In the pages of newspapers & those soon-to-be-obsolete & now
Long-forgotten journals

Of pure ego & fear
Now when I pass the cafés on High Street I look into the eyes
Of the young women
& young men poised & ravenous
Above their open silver suitcases those slick shining slabs
Each the size of a make-up case

& I wonder what they now too have

Seen reflected in the liquid pleasure of those screens

& in the solitude of such

singular prayers — & I hope

The songs I hear snaking out of the open doors of the cafés

Remain as vague & nostalgic

& angelic

As they have always been & after all the worn fedoras

Of self-delusion

Give way to the urgencies

Of the night the generous beds & sofas of a making so charged

With pure nerve & desire that all the fucking

In every room of every apartment house

Along High Street will echo with the sound of Tibetan drums

& the heartbeat of this rescued century

CODA: AUTOMATIC AUTUMN

Kasmene was covered with the red dust of the mistral
The little blue pins of the pine needles were latticed
Like some unfisted riot of storm-blown swallows' nests
Along both of her bare shoulders

& as I brushed the day's debris from each delicate slope of skin

I saw the flush of some excitement still there mottling
& mapping the degrees of desire arising on her flesh
As she watched the winds rippling the fragile face
Of the lake & I suppose

I should have taken her right then to the cool sleeping loft

So she could listen to the little nails of the rain starting
To telegraph & tattoo the beams & planks of the ceiling
But I was too shy to be so troubling of such beauty
Though it was the first & last of my young regrets to fall

❧ QUECHUA SONGS

DOORWAY SONG

I.

Star-walker please
Come home

I have left my window
Open for you

& the bed is warm

II.

The door to the sky

Was bolted shut
By the lightning

Now a single island of
Honey burns

The single open
Aperture of the day

SONGS OF LOVE & DESIRE (I)

I.

Last night I sang you
To sleep
With a lullaby called the moon

Ah now this morning
Even before the sun
Look what has arisen!

II.

I wrote you a message
On the butterfly who lives
In your hair

Oh golden petals of pain
Why does she look away
Every time I come near?

III.

My rope is knotted this way
So that I will remember
All of the nights

I have lost to you —
& also the simple way back

IV.

Here is your name
Scrawled in the dust of
My doorway

Oh lover
What is it you came to tell me
That I do not already know?

DISTANT MEADOWS

I.

Do you see the fields
Of white blossoms
Below the steep face of

The mountains?

Little moons fallen
Onto the green fingers of
Our dead children

II.

The tears of the violets
By the path
To the ruined house

Make the cat's tongue wet
& the dawn dew slowly
Pours like honey across

The broken stars

III.

The acacia is blooming
At the mouth of every cave
& also by the lips
Of the stone portals we love
& as the blossoms pucker
The fires of the earth deliver us

IV.

Pale fish in the green pool
Of the temple cistern

The sky above you is green too
& your lifted belly is like snow

On the peaks above us & even
The once opened doorway of your eye

Is forever closed

SONGS OF LOVE & DESPAIR

I.

Oh lover
The wool of your blankets
Has grown coarse & rough just
Like your love

II.

I am living alone by
The river ever since
You left me & now

I think of you always

With such unexpected
Passion & joy I think
You should not ever

Come home

III.

The black dove was eating
The white corn below the archway

Of the stone wall where every time
I ask for your love you laugh

Your silver bracelets rattling like
The chains of your father's dogs

IV.

Am I the fire or the straw?
Roll over & show me again

Every morning we wake
Covered in ashes

SONGS OF LOVE & DESIRE (II)

I.

Did you know there is a gold crab
Wrapped around your arm

Like an amulet against love?

Yes I know & I walk so slowly now
& I swear I drop everything

I try to hold

II.

Like love the ostrich's egg
Remains a curious accomplishment

She seems puzzled as she broods
Even now over its future

III.

When you lift the water pitcher
Up to your lips like that

& smile at me for a long time
From the table at the end of the room

I am suddenly so feverish & thirsty I know
I may die

IV.

I have an arrow through
My neck though I know

It was meant for my heart
You were always such a terribly

Deadly aim

V.

The pear is so beautiful
I love to cup its belly in my palm

Your belly too

VI.

Goodbye oh my lover
Now that I am dead

I look out into the rain
But I know it is only

The rain
No one is weeping

No one no one no not
Even you

THE LAST PORTAL

Where has your mother gone
In the violet twilight

Where was your father walking
That night he disappeared

The dragonfly above you keeps
Stitching her reply in the air

The dragonfly below is resting
On the passing currents of the stream

*

The dragonfly promised me his blessing
If I returned his shadow

& I returned his shadow that cross
Shifting along my path

The transparent petals of his wings shuddering

*

My mother promised me
The cap she had woven of alpaca

& dyed the deep blue of the sky beyond
The mountains you know

The cap with the long flaps to cover my ears
She promised me the cap if I returned

To our village & the girl with peacock feathers
Sewn into her vest above her heart

Turned & said to the whole marketplace
She promised she would be my lover

& play the flute of our evenings together
If only I would return

*

But of course it was too late
Of course I'd already followed too far

That path that winds high into the peaks
That rise frozen with silence

Of course I'd already come too near
The narrow stone gate of the gods

That is awaiting each of us & I had
Already passed beyond human form

& the last portal

❧ LOST LEAVES

FOCUS

In kaleidoscopic focus the young girl momentarily shifts from view
Until rising in the maelstrom of naked bodies collapsing
In the turning cylinder of the lens

The luminous glaze of her lips seems to shame even the most
Weary of us flailing away at our daily disappointments
In love & desire & as she is lifted up

Along the mass of bodies to be borne serenely
Into the village she's also quick to see that some sacrifice
Is what's required to keep the stew of things succulent

& new & even the most flaccid flesh grows more taut
At the thought & even the limpid mind itself snaps the whip
Of memory along the spine as the wide wild

Eye of the body opens

HOMECOMING

There would be nothing
To tell them
She thought as the cab pulled away
From the gate nothing

They hadn't already been told
Or perhaps had even read of
In the London newspapers
& as she began her way down

The long walk
Beneath the cathedral arch of
Walnut trees lining the wide
White gravel lane from the gate

To the main house
She wanted to laugh thinking of
How little she'd returned with
How the bag on her shoulder

Held only the essentials one might
Take in the dead of a summer's night
When one was desperately running away
Not back again   toward any home

WISDOM'S SHADOW

Her mother was an elegant woman
Though plain who married often

& with great wisdom the men
Who would leave her the most money

& the fewest scars or so
She—the mother—had always claimed

Though after the funeral & the hateful task
Of cleaning out closets neglected

For years had at last begun
My friend called me to her mother's bedroom

& pointed to a mattress covered with brocaded silks
& knee-weakening lingerie but most dramatically

A pigeon-gray floor-length velvet coat spread to reveal
Its lining of iridescent particles of silk quilted exactly

Into a mosaic I knew well: Ravenna's Queen Theodora
Presiding over those last raptures

Of the soon to be lost Byzantium

HER PAINTING

In her painting called *The Tree*
Of Life (I know I know) my friend Solange
Had placed a self-portrait of
Herself at seventeen cocooned in rough

Bark ribbons & draped like some peculiar
Fruit upon the deformed lower
Branches of her autobiographical
L'arbre & when I asked if that was really

The way she'd always seen herself
A waif of chance   a petrified baby owl
Some cold blossom of nascence
She just looked up at me from her coffee

& said Some of us take what we can get
& some of us recognize the facts of our own fates
& those like you who can't are simply sentenced
To being death's tiny decorations

Those ornaments of pleasures almost past

SUNFLOWERS

I suppose that's the reason
Why for so many months I daily
Brought Solange a single stem or bouquet
Of sunflowers at least when the season

Allowed & after that photographs of sunflowers
Once even a plate from a flea market
Glazed with a field of entwined blossoms
& I believed those huge fringed eyes

Might persuade her that I too could see
Everything even the cruelty she preferred & as
The fall melted from its gold & amber
Of isolation into the snows of regret

I found myself alone at her favorite café
Almost every evening wondering what I'd done
To lose this last aperture of possibility
I'd seen open slowly before me & then close

With the finality of the setting winter sun

CLASSICISM

There was a time in my life
When nightclubs of the classic type
Seemed the only purpose of God's design
The wilder the scene the better as a rule

Go the theories of sensual chaos
At the Russian club called *Lara's Revenge*
I even had a special table that Stella
Kept for me & each evening as

I stepped through the oak door
I'd see her standing at the bar wrapped
In the coils of the feathered boa
She'd wear even in the dead of summer

As if the winds still came surging across
The Steppes & one night she said to me Sergei
To be hungry as a child is also to be cold
& some things never change even when one

Is married & fat & old

OF FASHION

I believed in those days
That most of the people I knew dressed
In some approximation of their own
Interior lives that is to say drably

& with little imagination
Just the usual washed-out earth tones
Of the newly dead
& so that evening when my old friend

Arrived at my hotel for dinner with
His new wife I expected this stolid burgher
To be well-matched by some dunnish nun
Yet when I saw her at the doorway

Wrapped by a coat embroidered in turquoise
Leaves the size of Venus's open lips
& soft against their background of red clay
I knew my friend had found the odd good fortune

Of holding his whole life rioting in his hands

BLACK FEATHERS

When you opened the door dressed
In nothing but your hat of black feathers
The red cascades of your hair
Curling at your shoulders & that smile

Of utter contempt just beginning
To fade to something more
Inviting as you bit the tip of
The middle finger of your right hand

With your lips parted so I could see
The perfect white book jackets of those
Teeth aligned so precisely
Beyond those swelling/swollen red doors

& a breeze from the bay behind me
Kicked up suddenly & the long midnight
Rippled like a fern's shadow
As you pulled your fingertip from your

Teeth to say *Come in* & of course
With each breath I could feel the black flames
& sexual weight of each extravagant
Quivering plume

WAITING

I am waiting for the star to rise
This evening in the sky

The one called Venus for its brightness
& pale reckoning

& if dusk erases the pleasures of the day
Then so much better the moon's wrecked pyramids

So much the wiser the woman who sets her sights
On the travels of Venus across the night

So much sadder the boy who believes the beauty
Of his love is like the beauty of his waiting

His patience & devotion rewarded unerringly
By silence & even

The sky knows better as it sends those scrolls
Of rain clouds to obscure his damp face

& the misery left by this new unwelcome knowledge

VEILS

The veils themselves are more dazzling often
Than the world they're meant to screen

& if you never again choose to twist the seven scarves
Of circumstance around your body

Like Hermès bandages or Byzantine tourniquets
To quell the simple flow of blood between us

Then I'll confess that tenderness is what I believed words held
Until I learned from you that tenderness was exactly

What had been bled from everything I'd said
The way a yolk's sheath of albumin illuminates

The black stones of a kitchen floor & if wisdom
Were a child naked in your naked arms then you too might

Wake still held by the mother of the air

ANOTHER KISS

It is instead the echo of a kiss
The vibration of the air surrounding
The moment before the collision
Of lips with lips

It is the solemn certainty of the tongue
Arriving without thought
But with enormous & admirable determination
& special drive

It is the hunger & the bark of hope
It is soul lifting the apple to its lips
It is the melting of the bones of the face
Into the bones of another's face

It is the robes of despair let fall
It is the pressed silence of the usual lie
Held just under the tongue like
A penny for passage to the land of the dead

It is the bowl of ragged scarlet tulips
Suddenly lifted in the sunlight
Like champagne flutes
To toast the simple rags of tenderness

Scattered everywhere upon the air